Momma Said...

By

Richard White
"Shake The Poet"

Printed in the United States of America
Cover Photo Richard White
Cover Design Christopher Michael
Edited by Sunni Soper
ISBN 978-1-7333152-9-6
Published by 310 Brown Street
www.310brownstreet.com

Shake The Poet

Richard White

Shake The Poet

The Rain of the Sacred Teaching Falls on all People
Those Who Embrace and Accept it
Find Themselves Swimming
in the Great Ocean of Enlightenment

-Ennis M. White-Robinson
(Momma Said That)

A (Westernized) short,
Japanese poem consisting
of 17 syllables (5,7,5)

Open Up and Speak
Momma Said to be Honest
Some things Must Be Said

My mama always said, "If you mad then say you mad." A prompt to be expressive. Even though she was the adult and the authority. Even if the grievance was against her. She encouraged the word—good or great or terrible or devastating. There's 11 years between the birthdates of my brother and myself and we each lived thru different eras of Ennis White-Robinson. However, there is no gap in the expression that she was the catalyst for. I salute your truth brother and am forever grateful for the writings you left inside the womb for me.
-Sabre Burroughs

v

The Contents

The Personal Secret Stuff

Family Trauma   7

Depression   9

Unresolved   11

Slammed   13

Purple Hearts   17

Exhausted   19

Hope You Understand   21

Talking to Myself Out Loud   23

Poems for Ladies

To You   31

A Year Ago Tomorrow   33

Just Like a Black Woman   35

B.Sweet   37

Cheekbones   39

X's and Ho's

Order of Ex   47

Vent Session   49

Maybe Worth It   53

Sexual in Nature

10 Minutes   59

Three X   61

She Can't   63

The Offering   65

Shake The Poet

Poet's Poems

Hold Me 69

Rich, White 71

The World 73

Heartstring Poems

There's This Woman 81

Love Won't Let Me Sleep 83

Fear Storms 85

Happiness Gone 87

Black Shit

Fade 95

No Colors 97

Tongue 99

Masculinity 101

Dear God 103

Aliens 105

Broke Nigga 107

Class Dismissed 109

No Laughing Matters 111

Crown 115

This Black 117

Richard White

Personal Secret Stuff...

Richard White

Family Trauma

Am I ok with my childhood?
I thought that's how it was supposed to be
I've got memories of being sent to the store for loose C's
Before I was old enough to be trusted to get groceries
Imaginary friends spoke to me when they'd smoke
To me, it was just a way to cope
They'd wait until I was asleep, not knowing just how woke I was to
the dope
Act like I didn't know
Black soot underneath the spoon, white residue on the top
Dish duty, even with empty pots, kept me busy when Pops had to cop
rocks from the block
Maybe that's why the block called him Roc...
Remember folks too high to "Hello" me, I was lonely
Decided that drugs would never control me, they were below me,
Beneath me, and where the rock couldn't reach me, came the hard
place
Found peace in an odd place by God's grace, God's face in my
mother's tears
I feel like I felt them
With she, we seeking refuge in Battered Women's shelters
The "Harmony House," switching schools, escaping, hiding
Fighting, lying, keeping secrets, learning silence cause, "You talk too
damn much!"
Kept quiet when I was touched... inappropriately, repeatedly
By a drunken friend of the family, who never practiced decency
And until recently there was still a piece of me that had never made
peace with me
Battered and abused when coke had mom confused,
I made a badge of ever bruise, never cracked
I knew that crack made her it's slave, so I forgave
Learned to let my tears stain the page
Soup kitchens, breadlines... I learned that from Momma
I didn't fear the dark those nights sleeping in the park
I was more afraid of reliving my trauma
Recalling... dealing with family H.I.Vs and A.I.Ds

7

Richard White

While teaching my baby sister her ABCs through Do-Re-Mis
College was bittersweet, feared leaving behind my siblings
Then found myself fighting someone else's war, before I could beg for their forgiveness
Two sisters had children, 1 married, 1 slain, her killer in prison
I was never there to witness, and maybe that's why I feel distant
The truth hurts like a mother fucker, so I've been lying to myself forever
Clever right
I had found better nights, when I would write until I had severed light and placed my dark thoughts between the lumens...
So, when turned inside out, I can find the human in my ruins
Proven to self that hell wasn't what I thought, when I thought about putting a blade to my veins
I wore shame like a jacket while developing a habit of acting like nothing happened
Imagine, being saddened by victories cause you feel sympathy for your competitors and enemies because empathy is the source of your energy
And this is barely the half of what I've been through
I have no better answer to give you, it's just too much to dig through
I just took every situation as a lesson, counted my blessings
So, when you ask me if I'm ok...
I'm sorry, but I don't really understand the question

Depression

Depression will leave you defeated until you defeat it
Hunger depleted, that pain... keep it
It ain't competing if you ain't taking a beating
I've learned, some scars are worth keeping
While they were eating, I was feasting on inner demons
Now that light I see inside of me, a reminder to me to be the beacon
I ain't lost my drive, my stride just weakened
I still behemoth – I still be seasoned more than salted tears
I'm still in there where they only hear my cheers
Where some snicker and jeer cause they fear the aura I wear,
burdens I bear
I swear, it's been lonely out here
Though I care more for them than they do themselves
I try not to dwell, hide, and try not to tell
Been holding shit inside, and I ain't been doing so well
Momma said, "There'll be days like this...
Said, "When you start thinking about stopping, stop thinking"
I'm just trying to stop sinking, falling, answering my calling with no
one to call when I'm in need of answers
Too numb to be angry when they blame me
So much peace was gained once I tamed me, but I ain't pain free
I wither and rot, I tether and knot
I bleed, occasionally drop to my knees, and plead
There are times that it hurts when I breathe – it's funny
People always see me when they need me, I'm easy to find
But whenever I'm in need, those same people tend to go blind
Can't say that I mind, cause this small circle of mine can see through
this smile I keep my pain buried behind
I was warned... to keep my enemies closer and forget closure
To let the savage within get more exposure, be the soldier
Before the emotional corrosion makes me explode
Holding it in, I'm bound to implode – when bound, must unload to
reload, ain't but so much to hold, try and control – demolition
Things fall apart – people die from broken hearts, yet kill from hurt
feelings
I've been weening off people to feel better about humanity

9

Richard White

Reaffirming my sanctity by being left alone with my insanity
Never have I met a Perfectionist that had perfected Perfection
But too many Directors lack the will to take directions
I remain an exception, treat pain like deception
It doesn't hurt... it simply reflects it
A lie worth telling, but never quells the swelling
So, I'm still learning to pay the health of my heart better attention
Cause there have been too many days I've awakened wishing I didn't
Though proud of what I've done, would never do it different
My guess is the fact that I'm consistent is truly uplifting
I miss living, giving the best of me, been blessed but need to give less of me to those who don't value my value
My volume was up, so if they didn't hear me, it's because they didn't care to
I live by a code that most don't adhere to...
I fear too... pain aside, practicing passive, passion for their protection
Relearning to recognize the God in my reflection
Depression... not only leaves a scar
If you let it... it'll make you forget who you really are.

Unresolved

I thought this was supposed to hurt me
I guess it just didn't hit me, I simply felt pity, empty
He's dead to me
"Here Lies…" again, as usual
I've gotten used to losing when expecting human decency, recently
He thought he was secretly keeping me in the know… or in the dark
It was only a lie when he would talk, speak to me
I didn't believe, but we've pretended like we didn't know
Hoping he would grow, that he would stop
I guess we were waiting for him to Pop… be a father figure, a man
Never lent a hand, but was standing expecting handouts
He must've forgotten our mother's bruises, stitches, and scars
That led to his stints behind bars, Absentee Daddy
Left me to carry the loads – my goals…
Being ½ the man my mother was
He let me down
Glad there was no riding bikes, flying of kites, catching, or swimming
Cause he'd let me drown
Time is money and for both… he'd take credit yet could never debit
Fuck the time it costs for an apology…
He's been sorry long enough

Richard White

Slammed

I remember the debating, the hating, stating ratings
Achievements, who's the greatest
Who's got that 'New-new,' the latest
Who's getting set up for bereavement, believe me, I was beasting, eating
Been to the top position, I was seated
A monster spitting, on my Conquer Mission, but I loved the composition
More than the competition, not to mention, no comp from my opposition
I was winning, penning pain and shame, while some seemed to spit for personal gain
It was a game, like loaded dice, fixed fights, had that 'Virgin to the mic,' shit tight
Others hoping to discover judges dropping dimes
Me, I was dropping jewels for the fools and confused
I was writing for the abused, reciting truths, for me... it was more than 'Win or Lose'
When trying to be God on the Mic, you've got to fill those shoes
Feel those Blues, let your words touch them and heal the bruise
Sometimes when you hear the News, you've got to repair their muse, uplift them
Fix them, most broken folks wear scars and won't forget them
My primary aim was never to entertain, for that I didn't train
Too lazy for rehearsing or altering verses, I just feared faltering my purpose
But only scores mattered, as a matter of fact, facts didn't matter
Then their acts differ, the chatter, the slanderous data
It was new to me, tried to commune within the community until I wanted out...
Then I was only spitting out that nasty taste in my mouth
Pacing about, still the one some don't want to face in a bout
I saw them raising a brow while I was taking a bow
Repeated, "I do this for my children!" like I was taking a vow
Maybe it was the way my naked aroused, crowds of clowns began to surround the crown

13

Richard White

My fear of drowning in sound began pulling me down
Poetry wasn't a hobby, she was a habit, a 'Have to Have it'
But I made it a point to never prostitute a piece for points
A Paper chaser... knowing anytime I, Shake – loose leaf, Poets lose
sleep when competing
When they started battling me, I was battling demons
Backstage with the laughter, but all I could hear was screaming,
meaning
I wasn't enjoying, it became more like employment
So, I slayed and got paid, surfaced before getting washed out by the
wave
Served, faced, learned from greats, some I ate, became one, trained
some, gave some direction,
Drive, diction, painted pictures to give them better descriptions
Pen still sick, I write prescriptions
Still Slam hard anytime I try to put my mind to, Slam God when I
decide to, finetune
But it's a Love/Hate relationship...
I found for a win so many became inauthentic, and I couldn't relate to
it
Even witnessed a poem about struggle fall to a jumble of words
about colors, sounds, space, and shit
Maybe I was biased cause the brother was my brother, and his piece
left his skin color uncovered
When it doesn't matter that you write tight... cause 'We' want that
Great White Hype
But me, I wanted to be like MIC, it was clear
Another black man failed to be judged by his peers, so when the
smoke cleared, lights dimmed...
The pearly whites of his smile and the gray in his beard disappeared
like he wasn't there
Or we were thousands in a room, but I was the only one who could
hear, it was weird
Though it was rare, I think for a little while I was scared, was on a tear
but thought, 'Why keep competing if it isn't fair?"
I tried to repair, reverse engineer, but no matter how much I cared, I
mentally wasn't there
I cliqued up for family, they cliqued up to slam on me

A war with words on reputations, instigations,
I weathered hating and faking of their congratulating
I could feel it in the air, they only liked for skills to be compared
Joe told me "It takes 10 minutes to smoke a square," give me 9 ½ I
can smoke every poet in there
On stages, pages, sheets – I'm a Street Fighter, Ryu, Ken
I don't need to stretch a syllable when I Haiku them, I'm proven
Vet, one of if not, the best
Why be a test-passer when I'm the one passing out tests
A few tried biting my style while I was biting their flesh
I broke hearts by biting right in their chests
'What Was My Name' they scribed while writing their checks
With all due respect, poetry became life,
Even my Wife – sitting in her Vin Wayne writing cinquains
I ain't got to prove I can do what I've done, now when I do do it, I do
it for fun
Son, run boy, run laps until you're as tired as I am
From carrying this weight on my shoulders and being slammed by
Slam
I had to say, "Walk away Shake," mentally... while you still can

Richard White

Purple Hearts

This is for the wounded warriors, to Hooah to quit
When the shit gets thick, treated every stab wound like a prick
From a rose bush, keep pushing, keep moving
Shoot and communicate, daily operations demand maintenance
Hospital patients, Patriots and inpatients impatiently waiting to
return to the footsteps of the enemy
Somewhere deep inside we muster up the energy, creating history,
the many we've lost
A moment of silence... for the Air Force Pilots, when enemy fire hit
the Coast Guard so hard
Marine battleships were ripped in two, emotionally scarred, like Navy
Blue,
The Naked Truth, is that sometimes it hurts more to survive than to
lay down and die
Sometimes, the Alive, cry in the darkness, no pride in this purple
heart...
The V.A. says the stress is post-Traumatic
Semi-automatic gunfire heard in our sleep, no feet, no arms
Foreign bombs disarmed him, limbless, lifeless
His wife just cries her eyes reddened, dry as she tries to cope through
the moments
Stay focused, it's never hopeless, until you give up hope, homes
broken
This medal is a token of American Gratitude
How the hell you expect me not to have an attitude
When children run up beside me, no positive ID, I see I.E.D, he tried
to conquer and divide me
If they try me, I'm gonna catch a body, so sorry
No glory lost, the cost was paid, by those we laid in those graves
We keep fighting though no longer walking the same, we keep
fighting on prosthetic legs
Left at home a newborn, returned to an infant he can no longer pick
up, throw into the air
Never ran a comb through her hair, his hands destroyed beyond
repair, eardrums snare
Tear ducts flare as rivers run rapid rolling from retinas

17

Richard White

We are victims, unprotected by a system that led us killing all even ourselves

These hearts bruise, these hearts hue like Blues, like disabled Vets with nothing to lose

Like reoccurring nightmares or Vicodin for the pain

When it's the Risperdal, and Trazadone that are making you insane

It's the 'Click' before the 'Boom' the prayer before we sleep

The souls of the physically impaired growing weak

For the brightest stars in the night who fight when life is at its darkest

For those who hit the hardest, who's lives became targets, survived only to be forgotten

This is our Medal of Honor, tribute to the fallen

Those who've had the strength to rise, our allies, may they rest in peace... until we rest

This Purple Heart I bear; I bear for you... God Bless

Exhausted

I am... tired of pretending, bending over
I invited no one over to kiss my ass
I learned to laugh a long time ago, a long time ago...
I was battling with depression, I was second guessing my blessings
Stressing, stretching for my weapon when the ends didn't meet
Back then I couldn't sleep – too weak to weep – could barely eat
Week to week like paychecks you ain't been paid yet
Empty
Tired of faking through my aching, I'm impatient cause my heart is racing
I just want to be complacent for a moment
Smiling in people's faces is my atonement for the things I ain't saying
My silence
Ya'll don't know that on the inside I'm violent
I just hide it well, and I'm tired as hell
I'm tired of people getting over on me, to those that owe me money
I ain't forget
I just legit, ain't putting my hands in shit
To get back my shit
I'm tired of crying – I'll admit
I've been sliding pain into my poems and bleeding through the verses
Oh, I know I'm an Alpha – Bet my X's and Ho's
Hope I remain the bigger person
I'm tired of being nervous – suffering from anxiety
Fighting this fight in me, I'm trying to get right with me
Cause something ain't right with me
Nobody even noticed that I get off mics just to beg someone to write with me
Trust issues...
I've wife'd motherfuckers that would one day stick a knife in me
They just wanted to spend a night with me
See what it was like being treated nice by me
I'm tired of mis-managed love and being taken advantage of
Tired of losing to rumors when I can prove 'em
Growing tired from choosing this movement, but I'm moving
I'm fluent in being fucked over, I don't hunch over

19

Richard White

I just cold-shoulder, I'm much older mentally
I pretend that shit don't get to me to keep my dignity
But shit pisses me off often, I wanna coffin and bag
I don't smash and drag cause I'd rather snatch and grab
I'm irregular, I'm imperfect – I'm hurting
Tired of searching for answers
Tired of HIV, AIDS, and Cancer
Tired of this America trying to eradicate my African
Tired of domestic violence and trafficking
I'm tired ...of tying ribbons
Tired from fighting with my siblings, while concealing just how tired
I've been of living
Tired of witnessing my mother suffer and covering my mouth
Tired of Cats getting close – then falling out
I told my brothers, I stopped competing when I realized there was no
one better
What I got to prove
But truth is I'm in hell battling devils of my own
What I got to lose
I've got no grievance with the Court of God
It's my job – as a Man to bring things back in order
I'm tired from fear of failure in the eyes of my daughters
Either drink the water or be led to the slaughter
But don't faulter, or fail, even when it hurts to inhale
Believing there's no curse in this hell, I'm just not well
And I'm tired of suffering in silence – so I've decided to try it
To write it and recite it, to no longer keep quiet about it
Shout it, scream it cause I need it
To heal, cope, and deal – I always wrote what was real
Now you can quote on how I feel...
Speaking my mind... I thought I'd lost it
I've just been exhausted...

Hope You Understand

I bet you've heard enough versions and sermons from different persons
that I've been living the life of the serpents, lies and diversions
I've been hurting behind the curtains, uncertain of my purpose
became a burden, I was nervous that I was undeserving to be of service
My Beauty still resides within the eyes of this Beholder,
you've just gotten colder, maybe I needed a shoulder over and over
or you just got bolder when you'd refuse
Or maybe I'm confused, and now you only speak when spoken too,
or maybe your judgement is choking you
I'm broken and we haven't spoken cause you thought that I broke the
rules
Fancy my scars and show this bruise,
if you were ever a friend of mine, our friendship would be too hard to
lose,
but you're too blind to find the truths
When chit-chatter hits matter and splatters data, it doesn't matter
that a factor hasn't been backed up, everybody backs up...
well, I'm gonna finish running this lap up after I'm back up
knock down those walls that had my back up,
and now I just know who not to call to ask for back up
I didn't care if the shoe fit, just didn't know so many people had the
same sized feet
A part of a Brotherhood, that if I'd jumped, they'd be ready to take the
leap
apart from the music and dramatic rumors, it's my wellbeing that they
seek
mostly everyone else abandoned ship, didn't know the water was that
deep
steep hills I climb, I'll grind until everything divine is mine
leaving no time to look behind
your tunnel vision is just about as good as being blind
Never-mind, I Never Mind, just let me mind mine
My Wife and I alright aside from the fights and life we're tight,
and all my daughters are bright like Stadium Lights and Hi-Beams
Still a career Soldier, so I got the job of my dreams
Still spitting, I'm still the captain here on my team
My spinal cord is crippled but I can still ripple anything I hit

21

Richard White

bottom line, you thought I was going through hell really, I ain't been going through $h*t
I can take it...
and if it ain't there for the taking I'll get creative and make it
I have a Castle to protect, I can see the snakes from my porch
Characters I can scorch cause I carry the Torch, but I thought...
my thoughts were like yours... wrong
Thought you'd be here when I needed you... but you're gone
It's easy to recover from being misunderstood
the hard part is when you're forced to miss... being understood
Hope you understand

Talking to Myself Out Loud

Have you ever seen the scars on a cancer patient
Double Mastectomy – stitches
Blisters on their hands and feet
You ever hug the one you love with H.I.V
Or witness your Mother – unplug your sister
After her boyfriend hit her to the point, she could no longer pick herself
back up again
Have you?
Have you ever cradled a rape victim in your arms as she cried
"Daddy I'm sorry I let him in! I thought he was a friend!"
You ever wish your life would end; you can't bend no further
Ever take the rage out on yourself because it's a sin to murder
Then pretend like you're alright, like it ain't a sin to perjure
You ever have your own shit to deal with
But real shit hits you real quick – cause somebody else needs you
You'll bleed you dry if you have to
Give to those who only have your back so they can stab you
You really thought they had you
Your friends ever range from
a lack of gratitude to those that claim you've got an attitude
When you ain't got it to give
Don't you show love to those who gossip how you live
Ain't you tired of holding back your tears and screams
Do you keep losing sleep like you fear your dreams
Don't you want to believe – it's ok to give up
When giving your all ain't enough
How much stuff, is too much stuff to keep stuffing and stowing
Do you keep going, not knowing if no one is going with you
You keep showing you're growing so that someone won't forget you
Don't you miss you
Miss who you were before the accidents
Before the habit of being passionate became passive aggressive
Before your only viable action was becoming a weapon
You ever say to your lord,
"I love her, I don't want my mother to suffer. Fix it or end it!"

23

Richard White

You ever suffocate feelings of vengeance by falsifying forgiveness
Inches away from your vein to end the pain
You ever thought you saw hope on the horizon, then finding just a stain
And you're waiting till that day comes...
You ever just want to break – cause you can't take one
Tired of never finding a way until you make one
You ever flirt with death so much you hurt yourself
Find glory in your scabs like you earned the welts
Do you belt and holler in seclusion and keep it moving
Do you find your mind, body and soul in ruins
Positive influence, negative thoughts and occurrences
And your 'Safe Space' is lacking the reassurances
You hide under gutters hoping to cover and conceal
You ever just want to escape what is real
Escape what you feel, cause you don't know how to deal
Basking in the brilliance like –
'I ain't ever failed my children and any of this world stands against them
I'll keep building until it kills them,
I've got a mission that requires living, taking and giving, forgiving and breaking
Maybe it's worth the aching
Do you ever need convincing or reminding
Cause no matter how fast forward you move, you keep rewinding
Pause... just stop!
Tell yourself, "It's ok to hurt, it's ok to cry, to doubt, it's ok to be human, and it's ok to be you.
It is not ok... to keep pretending that you are

Momma Said to Me
"There's Nothing Like a Woman"
And She Never Lied

Richard White

Richard White

Shake The Poet

Poems For Ladies...

Richard White

Baby, let no one interrupt your self-esteem
When in meeting, group them all just as they convene…
You've got that "AA" Group
Hands full of 'Applause and Apologies' not wanting to give you either
Neither nothing positive
Too negative to help you develop the picture
Your fire is a trigger, they see your vigor bigger and want to fit into your figure, figures
Sister you simmer and sauté, they're salty-
Teary-eyed, they hide their cries behind their pride
At times that's too heavy to push aside, so they decline and deny every invitation to ride
That gap wide – like hips spread
Pay Attention… To You
You've been seeking the approval of fools you've got nothing to prove to
Trying to find them, you'll lose you, who's gonna move you when you rock, Rock…
Erupt and disrupt the peace with every hurdle you leap, every personal goal you reach
Those nights you refused sleep, refusing to be weak or meek when you speak
When you dig deep to withstand heat
Pay Attention… To You
When that weapon heavy yet you keep that weapon steady
Facing each and every scary adversary, you are legendary
Caring for self, should never be secondary, ball in your Court…

You used to be afraid to swing with no one to go to bat for you
Learn to clap for you, you've got a habit of working magic
'No Matter' – Which Craft
From tonics and bonnets, potions and lotions
Motions of your hips, melodies off your lips
Makes mention of the meals you skipped to get seeds planted
Taken for granted, all you've given

31

Richard White

When you saw thorns being risen, lacking buds
Yet still found a way to love
While letting losses linger loosely, lowering your levitation, then lowering your expectations
Lying like you lacked lucidity,
Loyal to the losers who left you dangling when your spirits were angling down
Baby that's just dead weight that ain't hanging around
Pay Attention... To You
Don't look down tripping, your crown slipping
Forgive self daily, wake up, make up
Let your vibrance splash, classic face, not an eyelash out of place
Twice as much ass than waist, class, and taste
That beckons onlookers say "grace" you are great
If ever you need a reminder, let me remind you
Looking for 'You' in others will blind you
They don't define you, your design refined
And anytime you decline, that's fine too
Why worry about their songs when you've helped Hummingbirds fine tune
You Mother Nature...
As a verb, not just a word,
You deserve to be heard, healed, and honored, honestly and honestly...
You're a God to me, Listen...
Once you start forgiving and forgetting their fiction and friction, you'll truly start living Baby
Pay Attention... To You

A Year Ago Tomorrow

I am a victim...
Uh, a survivor
Of 524,160... I'm just going to say "rapes" cause calling them "sexual assaults" sounds like escapism
And I've been doing everything but... escaping them
No, no, I know, no I'm not stupid, I didn't put myself in ½ a million uncompromising situations
Yes, it was the same man
Is that supposed to add to or take away from the humiliation
I don't have a drinking problem, I'm self-medicating
Cause meditating just makes movies of my memories and I already know who's in the credits
I remember it well
The taste, the smell, his swell
Deeper in hell with every inch... his sweat, his stench, his grip, "Don't Flinch!"
I kept telling myself, "Don't Flinch"
As our bodily fluids mixed like emotions, I was sick
I had... no control, no hold on my sanity as humanity betrayed me
I laid and behaved for my safety, hoping he'd perform hastily and just disgrace me
Here I stand, stained with 524,161 bruised left wrists from being clinched in his fists
In that blackness, I felt powerless, and I've relived that battle every minute of every day since
His grip, his stench, don't flinch! His grip, his stench, don't flinch! His grip, his stench, don't flinch!
Haunting me, Harassing me
I can't remember him asking me if I liked it, but I'm certain of him telling me I wanted it
My stomach plummeted, I grew nauseous, I'm much more cautious these days
After learning how this game of life needs to be played
I don't want to be saved; I just want to be free from danger
He wasn't exactly a stranger
Some friendships feel like home until you're home alone

33

Richard White

Yet, I don't go out no more...
Better to be considered a bore than a whore
I mean, I did everything they said, "changed the way I dressed, smoked and drank less"
They said, "Learn some jujitsu. Get you a Ginsu to stick with you. Double check the locks,
Keep you a Glock you can get to. When you hear a knock, No... stop, drop and roll
Yell, "FIRE" cause then somebody will listen
524,162 times I've failed to escape from this prison
My life ended with this life sentence
I've tried to imagine... I could reimage my image, but what would that look like
When every vision I envision forces me to remember when his member entered the center of my soul... the 1st time – and I'm reminded... of his grip, his stench, don't flinch!
I used to be thankful, he let me leave with my life
But when tortured with every breath I take, every single day
There are times I'd rather he just took my breath away...
I imagine that's the story he tells...
A year ago tomorrow... I'll have had the fight of my life
And I don't know if I can make it through another night
Even though... I've survived 524,163 reenactments of the worse kind of pain...
Do you like my dress
It has pockets...
That's where I hide my secrets, this trauma, and my shame

Just Like a Black Woman

It's just like a Black Woman to overcommit
To act like she ain't already dealing with shit
Concealing that feeling to quit with grit, she got tit
Drive in her stride, drying the cries from her eyes
Pride aside, in she – confide, she's down to ride
Though her insides been widened by all the 'failed when tried'
She tries to hide to stand behind – beside
I swear, she's cancelled on herself to help you a time or two
Give you her last without you asking, your happiness and laughter
she basks in
You're down bad, she's asking what happened
Like she too ain't mad and saddened, she's got a habit of being
battered, bruised,
Misused, confused on what to do, situations of lose-lose
Her Red bottoms ain't shoes... just foundations to blend in the
beatings
Her smiles wreak of misleading – but she's got you though
Just like a sister, sometimes mother figure
Going without to insure you have
Just like a Black Woman to secure the bag, just to give you ½ of what
she's got stashed
Filling her pockets with struggle just to empty the hands that touch
you,
Love you like life only matters cause you do
Just like a Black Woman to want a mani-pedi
But for others, hustle and bustle starts before she's ready
She juggles the heavy, reenforces levees when those tears come
Just like her to reach out to those she doesn't hear from
To nurse, ailing husband, at same time comfort her mother
Between laying to rest her brother and grandmother, battling an
illness
She just adds on concealer to conceal what she deals with
Just like a Black Woman to feel sick, to still get
She's cramping and bloated yet still going, showing – no signs of
slowing
Not knowing from where the next comes, till the checks come

35

Richard White

Stress and PMS, she be a mess
She's still a blessing when feeling less than blessed
Best foot forward while shouldering the burdens
Though hurting, she's still serving the undeserving while certain they
wouldn't do the same
Just like a Black Woman, refusing to kneel to pain
Chained and shackled to responsibility
Buries her self-pity beneath her dignity, she still shows signs of
sympathy
She still finds the energy
Ankles swollen, still holding it together
Still greet you like Sunshine in the cold and loneliest of weather
Can't measure, or gauge her positive push, prowess, patience,
passion, potential, promise or power
Watch her flower in a drought and still put fires out
Everything she nourishes flourishes
Just like a Black Woman to be sure with no assurances
Pure endurance, her performance is praiseworthy, poised
Just like a Black Woman to silence the noise, the screams, the shouts,
the doubts
Cause when roads block, she finds alternate routes
Routinely switches routines, leading roles
Feeding goals, freeing souls, fleeing holds when she's not feeling
those
And no matter how hard the job or how odd
It's just like a Black Woman... to be God.

She B. Sweet
She be strong, deep like roots
Tough like soles of boots, soldiers, troops
She be all that's lost recouped
She be the "Ends meet," that soup... for the sick
That candle wick, she be lit
Like the lights in this house, like never an empty mouth
Salmon, Trout, and bread loaves
She be the reason I'm prayed for, soul covered
She be mother... the reason I'm living
Momma been grand, way before her children had children
Momma be sick, tired, Momma be fighting battles in private
Momma would find it and provide it
She be whom in which I confided, even in my silence
She be love
She belongs... to a long line of children who're not her own
She be hurting, she be working
She be in business cause some of these bitches have no business
having babies
Excuse my language Momma, somebody has to say it
Sometimes some of them are too loose with who they lay with, it's
dangerous
The life of a child ain't nothing to play with
She be the anchor for the shipwrecked, abandoned and forgotten
Be providing a place for babies to lay their heads, while their moms
are out bed-hopping
John-shopping and coochie popping
Leave it to some of these mammies, these kids won't know family,
they don't know a daddy
They wouldn't know a happy if it weren't for Mimi
We had an understanding to be better than our parents at parenting
Apparently, that only applied to our family
Cause bruises tend to tell the tales that they already know what
abuse is
They tend to be homeless when their momma's new boyfriend
begins to act funny

37

Richard White

They aren't getting new clothes when their momma is spending that tax money

Maybe W.I.C makes me sick knowing so many of their mothers' prowl in search of 'pay me dick'

Momma B. be like, "you ain't got to pay me shit! Give me that child, child straighten your life.

Don't make them babies pay the price"

She be life, and she be right... every time

She be mine

She be warrior, she be beast

She be mother... she be sweet

Flowers For My Mom, whom the kids call "B. Sweet" (may she rest in peace), and Mother-in-law called, Miss B/Mimi.

Cheekbones

Pages and stages can't handle these changes
I thought time would vanquish the anguish, but pain is ageless
I've made mistakes while climbing the ranks
Thanks for the lessons, learned to create the weapon, found myself
Outside the box, had to think free of the chains, I'd bound myself
Outside I boxed, had to defend, and protect, battles fought with myself
Decided to pray but what's odd is...
Momma always came through before God did
At times, I believed they were one in the same, she just changed form
Tears to cheek was a rainstorm, her voice...
thunder heard when I'd brainstorm
I miss mine, try not to cry over missed time
I've got stories with no happy endings
Surviving storms beneath cracked ceilings, is exactly how I'm feeling
But I'm dealing with my demons the same way I've seen Mom do it...
With a smile
As puzzled as a jigsaw missing half the pieces, only half the man that she is
Although I'm striving, I'm dying to feel alive again
To feel what I'll never find again, still searching, still hurting
Still learning that the loss of loved ones lingers, lasting life long
Strong enough, maybe
I've watched cancer turn my mother into my baby, never see this woman break
Just gashes and lacerations, resiliency was amazing
Yet her greatness caved in, and I could do nothing to save her
Her losing her vision, made me see clearer
Losing her in the flesh, I fell in love with mirrors, these cheekbones...
I smile to raise them, to praise her
Grateful I was there to feed her, change her, not leaving her in the hands of strangers
She loved to talk, had a fear of the dark, yet was blinded and silenced
And I don't like the irony in that
Within her final sleep finding peace, I'm left with promises and secrets to keep

39

Richard White

Noise to make, pictures to paint, and curses to break... and it aches
I don't know where to go to escape this pain, but these cheekbones...
Much like hers, show signs of rain

Never Hold Your Tongue
If You Got Something to Say
Momma said, "Tell it!"

Richard White

Richard White

X's & Ho's...

Richard White

Order of Ex

I was once asked if I could explain my Ex's without exaggerating...
Well not exactly, it's magic
I've mastered making dumb shit vanish, then take advantage of their absence
In their absence, I've managed to become a Manifester before a Man Who Festers
Forget them
Forgiveness is for self...-ish, I had to apologize
For providing and ghostwriting for liars, fueling their fires
Grew tired of being the survivor, revivor of my reputation
Tired of the aching and heartbreaking
Silently suffering and buffering between bulletins of bullshit behind bad breakups
because business... never stays personal, when the person who owes you the most, just keeps taking more from you...
I could've become savage with what I managed to salvage
So, I apologize for holding the truth
When I could cock it, aim it, and shoot
Forgiving myself for holding hostage the proof
Biting my tongue, lying to myself by pretending to be numb
Knowing not allowing myself to feel was worse than not allowing myself the time to heal
I had to deal with that
Let me explain my Ex's without the use of examples or excuses
Just how I've handled the bruises and misuses before handing them deuces
Being naïve and foolish, pretending to be clueless
Allowing me to reflect on the neglect and disrespect that I'd accepted, I was infected
I had failed myself every time an Ex was tested
Negative became a positive, and I was positive
Of what she was doing before it was proven
But I kept moving my boundaries and walls, hoping she'd fall after every stall...
She wasn't sweet, she didn't shine, she was no world of mine, barely emotionally around

47

Richard White

So, when my eyes cried rivers, she wouldn't notice if I drowned
I crowned and kept going, kept growing
I won't be a sap or slave to no one
No longer masking my pain with shame
And I don't have to expose the lies she exclaimed
Especially since her loss worked out for my gain
Unphased, being given a misnomer by the misinformed and misled
Prepared to be misjudged by those who only know what Miss said
My story has been misread, mis-taken by many who've missed chapters and missed pages
Never cover to cover, trying to cover me and who I'm coveting
Hoping to uncover and discover a cover up, to keep from covering their mouths
The whispers are so loud, you can hear my pain...
And yet, look at all I've gained...
So, when questioned about my Ex's... There's no need to explain

The Vent Session

You don't like talking to me
You no longer have to, I ain't mad at you
I just find it pathetic how you be acting with that attitude
I be asking Self if your intent is for me to lash back at you
Or if your heart is incased in too much ice for me to batter through
Truth to a liar, nothing worse than a love that's expired or to feel
hatred from a mate you admire
Fighting is tiresome
I just want us to communicate better
Maybe you should try it some
Voices of doubt in our heads, I'm trying to quiet them…
But they're becoming more a part of me
The more that you're apart from me
And you wonder why I never believe there's truth to your apology
You'd rather take a pause from me, this ain't how it's supposed to be
You just take me off and hang me there
I thought I was more than just clothing and upholstery
I want to feel like a husband and a man, but you can't understand
that
In this fight I'm undermanned, and I can't understand that
I'm reaching toward your hands, but you keep pulling hands back
It's like I don't stand a chance at ever bringing romance back
And I thought we were passed that
A trust was lost that I can't have back
But everything else you throw at me, you can have that
You don't want to listen to reason even though I have facts
I've been getting left back even though I'm a class act
You just seem to make things worse than they are
I'm trying to raise the bar, but you're the only one drinking
You keep assuming you know it all, but I'm the only one thinking
This relationship sinking, but you won't let it sink in
As if your love just died, and I'm trying to bring it back from
extinction
There's a difference between what you do, and try to

49

Richard White

But it's clear that you can't make the distinction
I'm going off actions, you're caught up in your feelings
It's causing these distractions, it's a pattern
You can't tell the light from the lantern
You don't know what being a match is about
It's a match, it's a bout
How is your fight, fighting for us
When I'm the 1 thing you can do without
You don't need me, that was clear in your words
You don't want me, that's clear in your actions
Now when you're smiling in my face, I can't tell the real from the acting
I can't tell the pain from the passion
Maybe I'm too drunk in love to remember half of what really happened
I tune in to Madden when I'm saddened
I take the long pass, you take a Hall Pass, we start heading down the wrong path
I'm watching for snakes in the tall grass
And as long as there's a small task, I can ask to add value to
Maybe you'll value me like I value you
Instead, you rise up whenever our volume do
You're slowly erasing me, like your whole plan is escape from me
Showcasing hate for me, it's plain to see
All you have to give are headaches and complaints to me
Making a way to get away from me
I ain't your 'better half' I'm the 'broken pieces'
What you'd rather sweep under the rug and stomp out
That's why we don't know what peace is
We can't see what "Us" are, or what "We" is
Just looking back at what he did, or she did
Fact of the matter is that there's a lot of crap that "We" did
Where's the truth to the forgiveness that we give
Funny, there's no "I" nor "U" in "Love"
Yet it feels like 'I owe You' my Love
And I can't get passed this need to ask, "What do you do for love"
Then again, maybe this isn't
Maybe that's why your heart won't stay, only pays me in visits

I feared you'll stray one day, so I began savoring minutes
I've seen it in your face sometimes, you hate you ever gave me them digits
I can dig it, I get it, it's simple arithmetic
Subtract me from the equation, then next step... long division
This ain't intuition,
This is what I envision when I sit and listen to your thoughts and visions
Our light, fractured by prisms, kaleidoscopes
I'm trying to find us hope, I want to climb, but you keep hiding rope
We're burning down, I'm too busy trying to hide the smoke
Business to ourselves, I thought that's how we'd keep it
You keep leaking secrets, then get mad when I'm taking up defense
You hit me at my weakest, then tried to act like you're speechless
When it comes to you. The thing that's so unique is...
You do things to hurt me purposely
Then don't want to hear a word from me
Unable to understand my urgency when I feel like we're having an emergency
You be lacking courtesy
Between the fighting and mind games, home has become a battlefield nursery
Keeping in mind, our kids affected, I get disrespected and digest it
Before trying to deliver my message
Yet my best is still unaccepted
Years invested, but it feels like you view me simply as someone to share a bed with
And we aren't getting naked
Sharing shells of ourselves and being forced to take it
The rings came off and so have the gloves
It's easy to see that you're no longer in love
We were the powers that be, until you removed the plug
Our connection was electric, we're no longer lighting up
Tend to be loose with the lips, it's disrespectful
Our conversation needs to tighten up
You can't stand the sound of my voice
Some things can't be fixed by force, but by choice
And you choose to lose me and I'd honestly rather if you had used me

51

Richard White

Then to have had me just to remove me
Truly you act unruly, love could've fooled me
In the past I'd ask for you to be fighting more
But it seems that a separation is all that you've been fighting towards
So, I'm left asking myself...
"Exactly what is this... that I'm fighting for"

Maybe Worth It

You may be worth fighting for
But the war is worthless
Won't flop on my belly,
On the floor with serpents
I have more of a purpose
Won't prostitute myself
I'm not a whore for purchase
I got seeds to water and nourish
I got the means to flourish
Don't need your discouragement or false encouragement
I don't believe in being hurt again
Character murdering
Haven't you heard of him
The faceless have been packing dirt on him
Even though they're lacking dirt on him
Who do you trust when the going gets tough
When the cobras in the clutch
When you're stuck in those ruts and ruins
When you're pained and your train ain't moving
When there's stains that came when your days became blued
When your frame came unglued, and your remains bore bruises
Learn to remove the phony and see how lonely you really are
No one really knows me if they tried to hold me from afar
Spilling tea, and they wonder why I continue to raise the bar
No chaser in my spirits,
I leave the doors and windows ajar
People may leave
Just don't think about coming back again
Even Lost Boys know,
Demons and blood suckers got to be invited in
Already vacated the corners they were hiding in
Scatter like roaches when the light shines
We ain't got like minds
So, they pretend they don't like mines
But only from behind my physical view
I heard the whispers, I was listening too

53

Richard White

And for any who doubted me
You should've paid more attention to who you were listening to
Wolves attack in packs
That's why it was you they were mentioning to
They may have thought less of me, but thought lesser of you
My ego died in a fire, I'm so down to Earth
I bruise easy and hurt
I'm bashful, I flirt, I've had my hands in the dirt
I know it takes work to make things work
But any one jerk can make things worse
I've shared my hunger and thirst
In every sermon every verse
I'd rather die than to be judged
By judges who've done no research
I ain't scared to get naked with you
I'll strip for the search
You ain't got to dig up my roots
I'll give you my dirt
Let me be the first to show you my worse
Guess I should take it as a statement
I must be fascinating
Fake people fell off and dropped out
Now they're mad they ain't graduating
That's funny as hell
Got me blushing enough to flatter Satan
People hid behind their masks
But I don't like clowns, mimes, or Jason
I noticed the changes
When they went from standing by my side
To standing across and adjacent
Passenger seats became vacant as soon as I became complacent
Hatred got away with wearing makeup
Things started to shape up as soon as they felt the shake up
They must hate to see Shake up
I'm the type to grab a rose by the thorns
Memorize every detail
From the texture to the sweet smell
Protect the bulb with a seashell

Cause I know that every nose that stops to smell roses doesn't mean well
I truly admire beauty and it's my duty to protect
I grew from a garden where flowers would wilt, and weeds stood erect
Where you couldn't eat on check to check
So, we fed on respect
I can't respect you for being disrespectful
You disrespect who respects you
Then you'll neglect who accepts you
I will build with anyone except you
If all you do is tear down, how do you expect to
I bet you thought you were special until I came and checked you
Treat you like I never met you
It's best you fall back or get forced to fall down
Cause if I'm pissed off, you're getting pissed on
Until your entire colony drowns........

Richard White

Sexual in Nature...

Richard White

10 Minutes

Just give me ten minutes...
Though it might take all night if done right
This is just my introduction, when hugging turns into rubbing and touching
You'll love the way I place kisses on your stomach, you want it
The pulsating sensation is patiently waiting,
Hands at your waist placing me where my face should be
Tongue chasing the spray you've wasted, I want to taste it, eat
Your hips raising to meet, pace changes it's too dangerous to switch places
Grip ankles, spank you, take you places you've never been
Bend over or sit on these shoulders, I'll hold you, origami fold you
Let this soldier take the blast, tongue in your ass, lick clit, kiss lips, I grip hips
You tense a bit, clenching your lips, my lips pinching your clit
I want you to want it as much as I do, tongue inside you
My warm mouth south of your border, following orders
Granting your body 3 wishes of bliss with every sensual kiss
10 Minutes, to make you cave into temptation, your cravings driving you crazy
I baby you, just like daddy should, you grab the wood
I'm stone hard but we're not going that far, raise the bar more your way, this is just foreplay
Collarbone and neck already wet with sweat, like sex has kept your breasts erect
Your breath is heavy, body ready, tell me how you like it
I'll scribe it with my tongue until you come
Knees weak, slurred speech, you peek, then I massage feet until you're asleep...
My face covered in your sweets
Be treated like a Queen as you dream the dream of being teased and pleased, mind at ease
Cream being squeezed from in between the seams
I lick you clean... it just seems like the night has ended, and like we've yet finished
Baby all I need is 10 minutes
59

Richard White

Shake The Poet

Three X

I dreamt...
you were in my bed, legs spread, and I can't get that head out of my head – face time
She was faced down, drowning in you
mouth covered in dew, in you and you...
caressed your breasts as I watched - voyeurism
I enjoyed the vision as y'all switched positions, bodies kissing
Hissing and slurping sounds mixed with moans made music, moved me – closer
My face in you, your face in She and we... ate like kings, royalty
My loyalty to her and lust for you, as you two became more acquainted
Painted love notes that spoke in body language
No explanation necessary, sexy – very
Derriere in the air, pear-shaped, apple-bottom
Me... drunk off the juice from your fruits
It was as if, this was the first time your body was truly touched, had your fupa sucked
Love handles grabbed with passion, abdomen spasms, as I'm smashing your back in
Thumb in your crack, your lips smacking in her passionfruit
While you're eating her rose, I'm sucking her toes – slow, with every stroke
Grabbing you by the throat, you choking She
She loving every stroke of your tongue, She cums, then you do
Pulsating as I moved through you, She - pulling closer to you
Longing to see how this tantra suits you, kama sutra
Her legs braid with yours like two sensual, scissors insisting on entering each other's incisions
As they glisten, I'm watching your bodies rocking by candle flame
My inner animal came to handle and tame
to dismantle your frames from passion, minus the pain
She mounts... slips down my tip, you sit on these lips
My tongue, parting your labia, tasting you, you wasting upon my face
Both of y'all's hips race faster than hearts beating
Me eating - you kissing - she - riding me and we...

61

Richard White

Came 3 times each at least, before She just wanted to watch you with me
Me – still throbbing, you engulfing, slobbing, bobbing - tongue running up and down my shaft
She cums – from touching herself to spreading your ass
Her tongue runs up and down your crack and back, and back
Until you sat on my lap, legs wrapped, strapped 'round my waist
Face to face, and I could taste 'Us' on your lips
She... licking your hips, kissing your dips, and biting your lips
Taking control like She's writing the script
She sips some wine, then sits on mine
As our lips meet and speak, she sucks your peaks, nibbles your nipples
Grabs your ass, as to ask you to move faster and after you've creamed and came
She came to clean you
Strumming your vulva, your meatus, taking you places penetration passes by and I...
I bury my face in her... and She purrs
She whispers... that, "Two heads are better than one, and this one... She prefers"
I dreamt... and I ain't been awake since

She Can't

She can't refuse it…
Got her stuck on this new dick, like a glue stick
I be trying to abuse it… when we do it
She said I should cum "tool bags and business cards" cause I
definitely know what I'm doing
I've got that work
I got that make you squirt before you get out of that skirt
That you want me to beat it, but I got to eat it up first
That, do I need to gag you with my shirt, you're screaming "Wait big
daddy it hurt" or "Oh my gawd your girth"
She can't get enough…
She likes it rough and deep, wants to be rocked to sleep
I make that ass "drop" and "leap" she gotta hop to keep pace
She gonna leak and waste before I'm reaching 3rd base
Cum on my face when I taste before sliding into home plate
She's into fishnets and red bottoms, but I'm just trying to make that
bottom red,
She be giving bobble head, that "too good not to swallow head"
better than every X-men
She give me that "Ms. Marvel head" legs spread, toes curled- she
bucking back, I'm thrusting… I'm getting stomach…I like to feel the
"breeze" when she blow, that crown and drown, those… burping and
slurping sounds is all I hear out there
She can't keep quiet…
It's like I penetrate the silence when I'm inside it
Its sounding like a riot, she releasing the hydrants and the sirens-
make that sound: J. Holiday… I eat that ass, brown and round, every
day is a holiday
Candles lit, perfect fit when she grips- love how she be biting her lip
when she riding the dick
She be trying to out- muscle this muscle and muzzle her mouth
But these walls can't muffle the sound- she's so loud it sounds like
I'm putting it down on a crowd
She can't handle this alone…
She be on the phone, calling other chicks to bone

63

Richard White

Searching for another pair of thick hips to ride the throne
She knows she's on her own when we get home, so when we roam, she prefers I make another woman moan, she only stop watching to give me dome... she say "two heads are better than one" as long as she's the one that gets the cum
She don't mind a 3-some, I'm pleasing one with my tongue
My head got her head sprung- She trying to make king-dome-cum
She can't stand the rain...
She loves my deep strokes as much as I love her deep throat
But it's like she can't stand the pain, she gone swallow when it spit- so I don't have to aim
She's parasitic ... I mean sucks like a leech, slurred speech
Even my balls feel the walls of her jaws and cheeks
My peak is steep, but she be taking it deep
She'd be on her knees if I weren't making them weak
We make fucking love, like we just love fucking
She says "Big daddy my cat "me oww"
But... she can't stop for nothing...
She wanna handle this dick like a champ...
But she can't

The Offering

I'm willing to bet that the best relief for stress is us sexing
So, let's reach levels, teach lessons
Just book the session, let's make a mess
Sweat through the covers, sheets
Let's start at that chapter where we let lips kiss and lather
Betwixt your hips, rather everywhere our lips gather
When I have you...
I just still want to taste your tattoos the morning after...
Still smell your aura in my mustache, a must have
I want to savor it, be forced to face that I'm your favorite
Freedom never felt so fucking good, no need to explain the understood
Frantic, I want you to damn near go into a panic when you can't have it,
Addict, unable to escape this energy
I want to make you want to masturbate in traffic anytime you picture me, get the scent of me
Picture me passionately pleasing, your pussy pulling my penis
Penetrating, plunging, your walls hugging my tongue while you're coming
Picture me kissing your stomach, navel, fingers strumming at angles just before you taste you
Let's entangle
Let me thank you, in body language – you speak that
Cunning when I converse with the coochie, I speak cat... purrrfectly
Imagine trying to swallow me whole, gagging between the strokes
Me grabbing you by the throat
Picture my face in your box again, a lack of oxygen
Breathing you while I'm feeding you, deep in you, teabag – steep in you
We can do whatever, its better together, no lie
Who can get you wetter than I, pleasure better than I, be my professor
Let me passionately study your anatomy, read in between the lines
Who can pull up on you and park just to make your legs part, like we both got walls to climb

65

Richard White

Have your mind blown while I'm having mine blown
Your wet and sticky feeling like Honey... I'm home
Who better than I for you to ride high on
Like frequent flights to cure those sleepless nights, who can freak you right
Quite like nature intended, the way you can still feel it long after I've been up in it
You crave for the touch, imagine me giving and yet you can't get enough
Imagine loving the lust between us, fucking you helpless
Pleasing you pleases me, I'm so selfless its selfish
Using your pelvis to expand my palate
My mallet making you mouth musical moans as I motion the ocean and seas
Harvesting below the horizon of your hymen, honoring your mind then
Reminding you what I can do, so deep inside of you
That I can see the other sides of you – make you crazy
Baby, let's say we play, may we
Can't resist, its as hard as I, yet I bet no one can touch you softer
Baby, maybe... you should take me up on this offer

Poet's Poems...

Richard White

Hold Me

Hold me... like we're both in hell (inhale)
Call for Momma, say a prayer
Don't make me into thin air, don't waste me
Use me, suck me in – don't lose me, fight this, believe me you can win
Help! Somebody! Please!?! Breathe!
Breathe... don't leave, we have time to make a confession, tell her she's special
Say, "God bless you" say less
You can't go out like this, what am I supposed to do, I can't be me without you – Breathe
Wait – wait – wait, say, "Thank You" stay with me
Say something, apologize... to anybody, somebody, Hell
ANYBODY, SOMEBODY – HELP! Yell, scream
Give me meaning – speak of secrets and inner demons while you're still breathing
Don't leave me like this, hold me... I could be laughter
Hold me... at least until after, love lays kiss on your lips
Tell the truth... I can be the truth – shh shh shh
Don't waste it, don't let asphyxiation take me
Taste me – savor it, this is your last gasp, grab your chest – clasp on to your breath, Me
Hold me, please... I miss you, say it
This is the time to tell it
Before you set me free, let me be ...Novel, Grand
Use me to explain the hard to understand, the misunderstood, I can be good
Hold me... until the right time, then speak your mind, then be sure I'm suspended in time, cemented
Make me more than honorable mention when mentioned, meaningful... Breathe
I'm not ready to go, don't blow out that candle just yet, I'm not ready for death
Tell them you're proud, as loud as you can
They won't hear another, "Happy Birthday" or "Congratulations"
Say, "I do" I would, all over again if I could

69

Richard White

Hold me, restrain me – fuss and cuss cause you're angry
Be honest, start complaining,
Let them know you know everything they thought they'd gotten
away with
Be gentle, give them potential lifesaving advice while losing yours
Hold me until you're sure, certain
And just before your hurting calls for curtains
Release me... let me fill the room and balloon
Let this air become what matters, breathe deeply, heavy
Before becoming as light as I am, make me Grand
I must be, for I am, the last breath in the chest of a dying man

*Writing Prompt: Persona Poem (last breath in the chest of a dying
man) 2 minutes in length. Commissioned by: Joe B. aka Element 615*

Rich, White

When I saw…
Caitlyn Jenner, supporting the Texas Abortion Law,
It made me sick
Still just a rich white prick, thinking with its dick, it didn't sit well with me
You're telling me, its damn near felony, a misdemeanor…
Leave her with a meaner demeanor cause you demean her
Cause you detest her decisions, I digress… She didn't request your permission
But, when you wanted to do, what you wanted to do
Almost every 'She' supported, you had the masses caring
You wolf in sheep's clothing, old rich, white man hiding under all that mascara
You're another Karen, Devil
You've got the people convinced that you don't really exist, you're just a myth
Like it wasn't you who led me to hate my brother, resent my mother
Like you ain't the reason my people don't get along with each other
Let's be real and reveal the scabs and scars you really are
You racist sons of bitches, or bitch-ass sons of racists
However we're supposed to say it, you Nation rapists, you sadists, Satan
You abomination that has bombed a nation or two, invaded a few
Blanketed the cold and gave us the flu
Wasn't it you, isn't it you
He who became a hero by rewriting His story
Some shit you just don't forget, which is worse
The dreams you've sold or the lies you've told
A land of the free
Had us believe that it was you who taught us how to read
You just gave us a new language when you enslaved us and was dishonest when you explained it
But that's the privilege put in place, power possessed
Come on coward confess, class is in session
Since you've been trying to get rid of me
Convinced sisters that Cis, Black Men are the enemy to remedy

71

Richard White

Walk with me as I jog your memory...

It was the rich, white man that didn't allow women to vote, silenced them when they spoke

Black men didn't have a choice in whether women were given a voice

Rich, white men decided what women did with their bodies, their babies

And had projects to project what the Projects would produce

Rich white men would poison, pollute

We find power and positivity, rich, white men would plunder and shoot

Pretend to be a friend, an ally, all lies, and all eyes grew colorblind to the white lies

Even before white lines snorted, distorted perception

Turning us against ourselves, a proven formidable weapon

Rich, white men told us we were less than, convinced us to count our blessings

So, we wouldn't count the lashings, created distractions

Cause distractions keep us distracted from the facts and taking actions

Distractions, keep us from hearing our calling

They've always stopped us from standing, cause they've got a fear of falling

My sister, I'm sorry if I offend you, I never meant to

I was broken by the shit I've been through, I bend too

Don't be alarmed, I don't have the means to mean any harm

Never had the wealth to be dealt a winning hand

I'm a man

I'm a man who happens to be black, I'm a man and I'm straight

So, let's get this 1 thing straight, I don't hate... Nobody

But everybody, has been led to hate me

By those old, rich, white seeds... of bigotry

Writing Prompt: Using YOUR NAME, take 10 minutes and write what comes to mind (i.e., Richard White/Rich White)

The Word

Somebody gotta be raw with it
Somebody gotta leave y'all in awe, lifted
With small remnants of the indigenous... homegrown
Scriptures and pictures of wisdom we were gifted with
It was written, how we keep forgiving for the forgotten and
unknowns
Minds enslaved, somebody brave uncovering the lies on every
headstone
Don't be defiant, go to war with these giants
They'll have you outlined, dying for pushing an Alkaline diet
Try it if you want to, you can have them hunt you or haunt you for
what you won't do
I've learned a long time ago,
you gotta be stronger than what broke you
Then I broke through, wrote few, spoke a few from an opened view
Now the winds change when I'm strolling through
I came to un-train and re-train, I'm game
Open your minds – I've got to reach you through entertainment
Let me *enter, tame meant* to break by force and fear
So, they took control of what you saw and everything you hear
So yeah, there's been collusion in the music to keep you foolish and
stupid, let me be lucid...
The truth is easy to come by, come by
Give me a listen, the cost, just pay attention
I'm gonna mention some interesting things without pulling your
strings
I've got dope product for sale Money
It costs less than the bail money to get you out of the cell you're
already in
I'm trying to enlighten by making the truths more inviting
Make being Under One Roof more enticing
We're fighting the wrong enemies -Beloved
Don't let the babyface fool you, I'll school you
I'm playing Chess Queen, let me move you
Kings may castle but the battle is much smoother when you're on
board

73

Richard White

Right? (write!) ... cause pen mightier than sword, I'm just speaking
Leaving inspiration leaking and deductive reasoning
Gotta keep our people thinking, I'm creating for change
Lives saved and minds changed
In my crosshairs, every target hit
Unlike when the Blind aims, you can see the tar get hit
Stuck on stupid, who's leading you
Food for thought, but who's feeding you, leaving you starving-
Artists got the hardest jobs; we speak life into Atom (Adam)
Spoken word, spoke the word ... Higher Power
That's why they don't want you smoking herb, Fire Flower
I'm just planting seeds, I'm just snatching weeds from gardens
I'm just honoring the Father by being a father
Created in His image -I Am- like my father
From the Architect to the Author, a Martyr for a Mother
I only exist to uplift my sisters and brothers
With success stories of over-comers and survivors
Providers, fighters, and writers, and I'm dying to be heard
Vowed my soul to my children, but to this world... I leave the Word

If She is the One
That Won't Make It Easier
Momma Said to Love Hard

77

Shake The Poet

Heart String Poems...

Richard White

There's This Woman

There's this Woman that I love...
We don't have the best situation, but the relationship works
She's been my sunshine through seasons of hurt
She's been through the worst
But somehow has become my sanctuary, my church
She don't even know her worth, her value
When the voices in my head get too loud, it's only she who turns
down their volume
And I don't think she knows...
That ever since she began walking through my life, I've been wanting
to kiss her toes
My lips longing to embrace every petal of her rose
I want to be every high note in her Love Songs
The muse to her Love-strong
The reason... Her love strong
I've made mistakes but ain't ever loved wrong
She's more than alluring eyes, thick thighs, and paradise on the inside
When Unicorns fall in love with Dragons, She is what happens
She is Black Girl Magic and Passion
When my mind was confined to a room, walls padded
She gave me a New World to inhabit
Showed me that Tragic... You can come back from
She asked "tell me about where them daggers in your back from"
She says, "When tears fall from your face, I want to be in place to
catch them"
She says, "Baby, those wars of yours, I'm sure that WE can combat
them"
How do I tell her that I wish I had met her
Back Then
I don't think she knows...
Our connection is cosmic energy, perfect symmetry, chemistry
absolution
If this Woman isn't the answer, she's damn sure the solution
The Crashed System rebooting, the proof of the unproven
Hips in motion, she is movement
Lips in motion, she is music

81

Richard White

Sexually plays my pipe with perfect acoustics
Now I know how stupid that sounds...
But y'all don't know how beautiful, that sounds
I be gripping and grabbing her abdomen
The part that she calls the flabby skin
Just to show her that I want more than just her heart, but the beauty
it was packaged in
She is ravishing and I revel when ravaging
Wanting to love her better, got me practicing
Almost ready to die, just to come back again
For her to have my back again, for me to attract her heart from the
start, before either of us met the dark and heartless
I've wanted and wished, we'd started this long ago
I don't think she knows...

Love Won't Let Me Sleep

Love won't let me sleep...
Leaving me too weak to reach beyond these bleak thoughts
Old lies I used to speak haunt me
They're taunting and I'm wanting it to stop
So many tears dropped, my personal bubble is a tear drop
I'm still waiting for the fears to rot
Trying to redesign the future I'd wrought... so hard for
Bare knuckle, worked so hard for
The lore I've gained is nothing compared to the pain I've caused
Wishing I could hang my most flawed flaws
That I could draw the 'Perfect Picture' a little clearer
The 'Picture Perfect' I never saw it drawing nearer
Like the way I saw my fall while staring in the mirror
Love won't let me sleep...
My mind is racing, pacing forth and back
Nightmares of when I'm facing toward their backs
and right there is where I lose faith toward their acts
It is in that moment that I awaken
Finding myself laying naked
Stripped of doubt and sin
but alone and without the warmth of them
I've paid this price
But never bought a friend
I'm making change, without the time to spend
You ever feel like...
Heart starts to harden, and your heart beats start drumming knots
into your stomach
Right before your stomach plummets
Facing another set of obstacles, do you 'Stay the Course' or run it
Count backwards from a hundred
Too afraid to fall asleep, don't count that Sheep, you'll become it
I'm still searching for a Peace to become One with
Love won't let me sleep cause I miss it
Searching for a means to fix it
Risk it, never again will I
They say one's Will, will die right before their eyes

83

Richard White

A feeling you can't hide or disguise
A feeling I despise though never met
Have no desire to
For the weak and meek who have found enough of a peace to sleep...
I admire you
I'm hunting Fear, for Fear is the beast I'll eat...
and I still have work to do

Fear Storms

When you don't fear storms coming down
Because she makes Thunder rise
She still gives me butterflies
Like my Mother cries for my life to be right
But she's the light that makes me appreciate sight
That dream I dream each night
I can't sleep tight, so these nights are deep fights
Until she walks through my visions
Her voice calling my name and moaning, so I listen
Take my position
Her silhouette is dripping wet
Maybe my imagination stretched to us having sex
Her hands on my chest, lips on my neck
She wanted love to be made in the spirit
I'm always happy to oblige
I close my eyes and she comes down and rides
Braiding my fingers around her waist, caressing her hips
Then she kisses from head to toe and back to the tip
She vibes into my mind, surges my urges and desires
To keep the fire lit...
She whispers to me to, "Wax It"
Burning the candle at both ends of the wick
I thought it was sleep paralysis, assumed I was having nightmares
But when I'm trapped in this state of Freedom
I stop thinking about breathing......
There is only she and this spell
Poisoned, I gripped the thorns, so now I belong
Stronger I become but powerless in her presence.....
My reign reduced to fossils and relics...
If you find any signs, dust it off and display it
It's probably decaying
She became the direction and the way
The work and the play, listen and the say
The warmth I feel at night and the heat I embrace at day
God-like.....Took a fly and created a Dragonfly
Then gave me wings and made this Dragon fly

85

Richard White

Yet, with all her power she still has tears.....
Tears that I will invest years to wiping them from her brow...
She may be the death of me, but same time best for me
So long ago, my eyes missed what Faith would have noticed
Missed opportunities for approaches
Bitter moments, so focused on what we thought we wanted........
Now I'm a junkie....Mirtazapine, Zolpidem and Eszopiclone fight my insomnia
I need separation from the sleep deprivation
Cause I have to see her again
Hold her hands, taste her lips,
Gaze in her eyes, embrace her hips
We still got a world of nothing to discuss....Just us
I'm tired of missing her
Too tired to sleep, can't rest my head, my thoughts, she is peace, she is paradise, heaven....
She is my Blessing
.....And without an infinite supply......
I fear I'll just watch myself die.

Happiness Gone

Where has she gone, she belongs here, disappeared
Misplaced from your face, a space now vacant and dark
Traces of an aching heart, like castles built with sand
She doesn't stand for long, man may be wrong, hands made she strong
But not strong enough to hold on, she's gone...
I don't care what they call you, Life is the only bitch that I know
How could she just up and go,
Go beneath your skin, don't pretend to not know where you've been
and who're friends or on who to depend, wounds mend
backbones bend and there's always a reason to smile
I'll never travel beneath your skirt; cause she and I make love every time you giggle and smirk
We flirt and it hurts to see you hurt
We work too hard not to see each other, she's my lover
It's like you're her mother and I promise to have her home before curfew
But because so many men have hurt you, you keep her hidden inside, imprisoned inside
I just want to see your smile, Momma I just want to see your child
and walk her to where the clouds meet the ground,
Where the Sun and Moon play peek-a-boo with the stars, I just want to be where you are
Before too far becomes too late, I hate to see you this way
When there's no grace upon your face, just the place where your distaste is placed
Why waste an Angel face on devilish bullshit
You're praying for a change with devils in the pulpit...
Prayer works, know when to get off your knees, God ain't looking for a blowjob
It's your job, to walk that extra mile, let's have a child through laughter
Name her, 'Happiness Ever After'
What could possibly matter more... why are you fighting wars with yourself
Why is your self-esteem living beneath her means

87

Richard White

She doesn't reach for dreams or believe she's Queen
She believes she needs
And I be he who is too strong of a dosage of all the wrong components
She doesn't know it, but she is her own strongest opponent
If she would take a moment and own it, learn to control it, maybe she'd notice she was golden
Instead of holding on to hopelessness and unhappiness, your happiness makes you happiest
Smile for me Baby, if not for no one else, smile for yourself
Take pride in that shine in your eyes, I don't mind if you do
Just for you to see what I see in you, I'd go blind for you
Finding myself crying for you so you won't have to waste the tears that race down your face
After this storm, I'll wait for your smile to replace the rainbow
And love your smile, until your smile becomes your halo
We live and love on borrowed time, she still owes me change, I always paid attention
I refuse to let her walk out on our friendship
I'm making smile support payments until new laughter is born
Tell me my love... where has your happiness gone

Momma Said, "Be Proud,
You Must Understand Your Worth
Cause No One Else Will"

Richard White

91

Black Shit...

Richard White

Shake The Poet

Fade

Do you know why they dread locks
In fear we may Bantu Knots
Bolas ... Fists, arm ourselves
Do not fret, for even in death, we are not done yet
Eliminate threat, we must protect...
Senegal... do a man's job – Never, back down
The King lost his crown the moment he sat down
Rise -like roots, snatched from the Earth
It hurts, like hanging fruit, they aim and shoot
There's anger in truth, endangered my youth, proof
That my melanin made my Mother a Martyr, my Father forgotten
In the name of Jesus, crossing T's for every EYE they've dotted
Abusing our benevolence, our kindness for a weakness
Convinced to turn the other cheek, while they peek at which side cuts
the deepest
You can't... dream of better when you don't know what sleep is
"Stay Woke" that's the mantra, we do the contra
We be the Somali, the Mongo, the Kongo, the Igbo
We be the Hausa, the Xhosa, the Fulani, the Mande... the Sandawe
And we... we be everywhere, from Niger to Zaire, our hair
Strong like backbones and calloused foot soles
We've marched, the starving and the parched with broken hearts
We've bled art, cried music
Sweating bullets to have our work turned against us
Drenched us in blood and lies
Turned us against our loved ones, watch as we kill ourselves
This is hell, and the God is not responsible for its creation
They gave us the Savior after they created the Satan
Dark is to light like, day is to night like, pray is to fight like, blind is to
sight
We forget that read is to write like key is to kite...
If you reach high enough... there's power above those towers
Cowards know, so they keep you slow-stupid, clueless
You don't know what to do with, you lose it
They steal it and abuse it, reward you with gold caps to chew with

95

Richard White

Your value- ain't as priceless as your life is until you're lifeless
Pay for your silence, cooperation
As their corrupt invasions, co-opt our nations
Agreed upon enslavements, like voting – just hoping, praying loud
Like laying down, so lay down, pick it up
Afros; we're sunrays, Waves, we sunbathe, we're Sun made
And since they ain't of this strain, they made us strange
We've been conditioned into submission, it's all a sham Poo
Convinced you it's a friendship just before they scam you
And we forgive death, more than they forgive debt
We don't return fire by wasting racist breaths
We just tend to forget…
We tend to forget… we forget…
You know why they dread locks…
Cause they've watched us struggle to escape these shackles they made
And they're too afraid…
To catch this fade

No Colors

If I couldn't see color, everything would be black and white anyways
Shades of grays that range from light rays to the shade of slaves
Epitaphs engraved across every headstone of our graves
When I say "No Colors"
I mean, no more reds from bloodshed of brothers left for dead, no more signs to 'Stop'
No siren, lights, just HI-beams, brights, instead of whites, badges, and bad intentions
The white noise of facts forgotten, failed to be mentioned
Black holes of brown bodies that keep going missing
Black people picked, pillaged, and placed in prisons
White flags waving, or awaiting white saviors to save us
Endangered, strangers won't claim us, white power trying to break and tame us

What would be different, what would be different if color were missing
Would our music be movement of the blues in our spirit
Would the greed for green still drive nations, would the face of anger still resemble Satan's
Bloodshot, what if in Black and White read
"Blood shot, Crips made slime of slime. More Black on Black Crime. Another reason to confine"
If I couldn't decipher a hue amongst the Red, White and Blue from the colors of abuse against the LGBTQ
Would the violets of violence still remain silent
When every bruise is being viewed on YouTube and the news
It seems these scenes are only seen by the few, while many pretend to not have a clue
If I couldn't see color...
Would I recognize the stale, pales from being unable to inhale, could I tell
Could I tell that their 'Green with Envy' made them red hot
Wanting to beat my black blue
Would I've seen that white lie, that in fear for your life you decided to shoot

Richard White

Would I turn a blind eye to watching recordings of the truth, would I too ignore the proof
Is this what it means to not see color
Is it to pretend that the yellow bellies of white supremacists don't exist
Is it, is it to forgive and forget
Or is it the pink slip you get when your black ass just ain't a fit
Is it to act as if we don't know about the gold they stole to get rich from the land we call Mother
Could I recognize my brother
If I couldn't see color

Tongue

If you believe there's power in the tongue...
How can you call your son - a Nigga, the woman you love – a bitch
Why you be saying dumb shit
When speaking ill can kill one's will
Peace, be still, don't part your lips, mouth – please be still, please at least be real
Heal before you deal out some shit that you don't want to get back
We shoot off at the mouth, then forget about the kick back
There are worse things than a 'lick back' from broken hearts
Get torn apart, alone, and dark, no one to talk to cause you tend to bark
Shit, just say what you mean, don't just be mean when you say shit
Save it, your tongue rips like the whips they once whipped slaves with
You speak of death, with all the negative you're saying, praying less
Does your conscience ever weigh-in
Day in, day out, out of your mouth shouts obscenities leaving enemies instead of friends-to-be
You tend to be harsh and dark every time your lips part
Wondering why it's always around you where the shit starts, you could mend hearts
Instead, you'd rather lash out and let that trash out
Why you keep saying that you can't, submitting, it's ambition crippling
Playing victim, a simpleton, why not speak higher of self
Why not name it and claim it, why not get naked, explain it
Instead of creating hatred, aiming, and spraying when you ain't even got to say shit
Making shit worse when you converse, rewrite that verse
Don't damn the church cause you're hurt, tell the truth, shame the devil, level up
Digging holes for yourself, you should put that shovel up
You slash, stick and stab with every jab
Speaking illness into existence, creating resistance and distance
Yet you wonder why nobody answers when you're asking for assistance
You should think about it, sleep on it, before you speak on it

99

Richard White

Exercise what's right when exercising your rights
And remember you ain't always got to say something
And if you ain't got nothing nice to say...
Then don't say nothing

Masculinity

They say, "Only the maternal matters cause the paternal pattern is absence"
I broke that
"I'll give the world to my children"
I spoke that, you can quote that
Generational curses
I broke that, hurt back and migraines
Out-thought life's mind-games
Struggle and strife – I survived that
Hurdled every obstacle I arrived at
That's Black Masculinity
I only lack what Massa' limits me
Equality, opportunity
I've got drive
Even when Cops pursuing me, try and ruin me
I'm a pillar in my community
Head of my house
World wants to silence me
Shout when I open my mouth
Call me aggressive when I'm expressive
They tend to teach me a lesson when my weapon is just a message
I keep stepping, I keep trying
We keep dying in these streets lying faced down
While White-fragility erase Browns... the Blacks
Mass killing me
In the name of 'Toxic Masculinity'
I ain't got the right to be angry, paranoid, and frightened
I ain't got the right to react like I'm fighting
What you expect
My masculinity protects, chivalry at its best
Only thing toxic is toxicity
That shit don't exist in me
It's specifically designed to decline my kind in the eyes of the blind and naïve, easily deceived
Another label provided by White Fragility that too many choose to believe

101

Richard White

Masculinity is missing, Men soft, pisses me off
We're lost like we've lost, when a backbone is all it costs
Masculinity is the opposite of fragility not femininity
Now we've got our own women stripping us of dignity
Perfect strategy from our enemy, watching us wasting our energy
All lies, allies they pretend to be
Masculinity is Pride in finding Bride
One doesn't become toxic because he disagrees with a man being
rewarded and celebrated as Queen – when so many of our Women
have fought just to be seen
It seems – we can't stand behind them both
Cause somebody gonna 'bitch'
Somebody gonna complain, like there ain't no deeper pain
Make like they can't understand what you're saying, cause what
you're saying ain't the way they want you saying it
Now that's toxic ain't it, aim it elsewhere
Like the welfare of our people and common evils
Like the toxicity beneath the steeples
Or the elected, wealthy, and regal
Manhood, isn't toxic, it's endangered
Increasingly becoming stranger instead of stronger
Manhood gets you backed into a corner, you're a goner
They must kill and destroy you, don't want to employ you
Rather enslave you the way they used to
Masculine – is Father Figure, provider, protector, lover of Mothers,
daughters, sister
Does not lift fists to hit her
Masculine men still exist… and we find your language –
Just as offensive – when you call us toxic
Apparently, some of you are toxic enough to be experts on the topic
Masculine don't stray from gay to straight it ain't hate
Masculine is safe for our women and children
Masculine is the Head, they wish to decapitate, exacerbate
Mistake the identity of
Masculine is not the warmonger, or whoremonger
It is the roar of thunder, the strength of gentleness
The perfect complement to the strength of the feminine
The power of our women and the God-ness in them

Dear God

Did you hear the traffic when the action of trafficking Africans was in fashion
When the back lashing was considered 'passionate punishment'
Did you admonish them, or abandon us, stranded us, strange lands – no freedom here
Black Boys don't cry – but we've freed those tears
Did you 'FREEZE' those years... decades, centuries of oppression, slavery, and ism's
'Filling your house' – did that mean prisons
Did that mean the harm of women and starving children
Lord, there must be some part I'm missing – "Dear God"
Did you hear them claim that in your name, they came upon the wisdom to form this system
Was your line busy, when we'd call upon the Savior, when we're in danger
Is this how "Father" came to be known as "Stranger"
Tell me if your hands were tied when they slaughtered tribes, or nations died, when the babies cried when being pried from their pride, when they would hogtie and divide, decapitate, degrade
Were you with the Angels playing Spades, when with clubs they came to crush our hearts for diamonds
When the mining turned to bombing
Was your silence during the violence, a calm before the storm
How much more must we mourn, how much more must be poured, how much more must we endure before you cure these ailments
Have you been watching since the beginning or are you just catching the tail end
Lord, some of your creations have made Hell here – "Dear God"
"Lam Yalid Wa Lam Yulad" (He never begat nor was begotten)
But it seems that He's forgotten that His children are downtrodden, cattle-prodded, raped, and shamed, beaten, maimed, and renamed
Unfairly incarcerated, wrongly enslaved
Yet we've behaved, waiting to be saved... By You
We've learned to "Forgive and Forget" – Just like You... "Dear God"

Richard White

Aliens

A man asked me if I believed in Aliens... Fuck Yeah!
Once, I had a Dream... that Travelers, Explorers, Astronauts, stumbled upon some new land,
Ran in to some huge and hued man, huge hands
Then they saw how he ran... "Goddamn!"
Staring in awe and amazement, some like they'd seen a ghost when another got close
He didn't run, but spoke in foreign tongue, made a connection
Pointed towards the stars and gave them direction
Then, taught Travelers to treat infections with medicine
Made with math, music and melanin, marvelous meals
The more they revealed, the more of their secrets the Travelers started to steal
While studying their young, who just seemed to be having fun
The Travelers thought, "they're so much bigger, stronger, faster...
What if they learned to master... (gasp) I mean what if they learn from Master
What if they rise up against us once they realize what we're really after"
An Astronaut said to an alien child, "Boy, what is your name?"
"Khalil"
"Kal El? That sounds a bit ethnic, we'll call you Clark"
And after renaming many, they started moving in the dark
Slaughtering their warriors, silencing their historians
Unleashing evil... punishing, poisoning, poking, and probing their people
A perilous plight, for they were unaware of the fight against these thieves of the night
Who took them prisoner
Those treacherous travelers were sinister...
Thought to take this Alien race to a new place
And since they were only 3/5 human, they only needed 2/5 of the space
So, onto 3 ships the travelers packed the alien bodies
On the U.S. Colony, N.O. Freedom, and the W.T. Supremacy
Stripped them of their land, laws, and liberty

105

Richard White

Destroyed their dignity with inequity and inequality
Yet the aliens... adapted to their oppressors aggressive tactics
So, the travelers adopted doctrine to block them, stop them from
achieving and seizing control
By making sure only grievance was known when feeding their soul
Only an alien here, cause here has never been home
The man said, "I only asked if you believed, you're telling me about a
dream, but have you ever seen an alien up close?"
I said to the man, "You don't understand, I've always believed in
aliens, ever since, I've been awoke"

Broke Nigga

There was once a time when death was free as a nigga could be
Unless he stole something, cotton field he'd grow something
Roll up and smoke something, the smoke coming
Sometimes you've got to choke someone or deep throat depending on the consequence
Might have to hop a fence for freedom… ain't nobody leaving
Nobody believes him but somebody need him, weed him out of the system
Put him in prison
Easier to hold on to hope when the boat is still afloat, coke and dope tightened the rope
It wasn't the hand of the white man,
But the whip that snapped across the backs of blacks that was the cracker
Master was driving slaves
Nowadays slaves are driving the whips, house niggas turned pimps
Field niggas turned wimps, real niggas turned bitch, bitch niggas turned snitch, trick or straight up dick
Sticking head in every hole, fucking themselves
More time in the hole than in the cells, the negative sells, so they put niggas on shelves
Top 5 greatest rappers alive died so the bottom 5 could rise, where's the pride in that
Ain't no pride in rap, just rims, Timbs and blue Yankee Fitteds
Every nigga done time, every one of them been acquitted
99 problems done got their mother addicted
On their way to getting riches and fucked a couple bitches, done left a nigga in stitches
Just itching to pull a trigger, popping bottles of liquor,
I remember hearing that ignorance was the most dominant trait of the nigga
Pretenders pretending to be contenders for a crown that was theirs to begin with
But it don't mean shit if we don't know the reason behind it
Absent-minded, blinded by the shiny bling, never seen self as King, "Ya Mean"

107

Richard White

Only street dreams for cream, a hindered self-esteem,
Especially when life's expectancy is barely the preteens
Seen leaving the scene, conscience unclean, it seems nobody seen
how we've acquired those things, those rings, those blings
Don't sing, snitches get stitches they say, so we don't say nothing
Afraid to be hunters, but complain of being hunted, WANTED
Philly-blunted, we're running from the FEDs, the Law and Child
Support, the trials in courts
Cause we were caught
Illegal abortions, street extortion, we keep scoring in the game on our
way to fame
My Nigga... Nigga you still my nigga, just remember when you get
bigger Nigga, that you're still my nigga, Nigga remember
When you throw it all away behind women, date rape, cocaine and
can't hold your liquor Nigga
You're still just a nigga, nigga freed from chains, you need to blame
self for the pain
The noose is off, but now the fool is lost
Act like we needed their leash to lead us, predisposition as a fetus
When they see us, "These niggas beneath us" is the thesis, cause we
must rise and realize the price of our lives is as high... as we'd like to
be
We're hanging ourselves from the tree, N-I-G-G... Aye Nigga we free
Even though we can't afford to be
We're broke Nigga
Broken spirited, we pay the price for ice and street life, but won't
wife a queen or fight for dreams, we were kings once
Before stuntin' became a habit, we were rabbits in this turtle race
Now our faith is misplaced, and they've erased our traits
Leaving a legion of lost laureates who haven't told their stories yet
Our blood may hold lock and key to the books of truth, but we won't
read them
Too broke to purchase freedom, spent our figures buying triggers as
snakes slither to deliver this message...
Nigga, my nigga, you're your own killer, we're surprised to see you
ain't dead yet... My Nigga

<u>Class Dismissed</u>

The case of Dredd Scott v. John F.A. Sandford... decided March 6, 1857, <u>Holding</u>:

1. Persons of African descent cannot be, nor were ever intended to be citizens under the US Constitution. Plaintiff is without standing to file a suit.
2. <u>The Property Clause</u> is only applicable to lands possessed at the time of ratification (1787). As such, Congress cannot ban slavery in the territories. <u>Missouri Compromise</u> is unconstitutional.
3. <u>Due Process Clause</u> of the Fifth Amendment prohibits the federal government from freeing slaves brought into federal territories...

Nowadays... it ain't even the Swastikas that pop niggas
Projects... they track and plot niggas, they like where they've got niggas
Policed... whips, pulled over, they swat niggas
Prisons already got niggas, so they drop niggas, on the spot niggas
Draft and trade, the slaves, they shop and swap niggas,
While department stores watch niggas shop
Shot niggas, boxed niggas in, nigga in a box, shot by Cop - we do not fit in
Nigga whatever you were, from whom you descended has been rescinded, changes
Amendments suit for your pigment, they hang fruit of your pigment
Bang – shoot at your pigment
No matter your back-bled contributions, you ain't backed by the Constitution
Until enemy shooting and they start recruiting
But that love only lasts until the system crash and they start rebooting
They start re-grouping – Professor and the Student
Doctor and the Chemist, Racists and White Supremacists
Now the rage in the machine is the product of the experiment
They've created a Zombie, and now they're in fear of it
Tearing it down... monuments

109

Richard White

A delicate situation for confederates in this nation
No invitation – brought, bought, sold into slavery
So nowadays we seek goals with limitations
African-American is a polite way to say 'American Imitations'
Tired of our protests and demonstrations
Tired of us begging to be treated equal
Tired of us begging to be people against lethal force and courts
Operation 'Let's keep these niggas fooled' program them in school
Tell them only what they need to know, never answer the questions
that they have
Why did whites hate blacks
Who sat before Rosa parked, what is it that Henrietta lacks
What's more valuable than melanin... is that why they're selling it
It can't be free... is that why they're cell-ing it, jailing it
If I speak too much of the truth, I'm told to give it a rest or get
arrested
We are all God's children, yet instead of your brother, you'd rather
protect your investment
Slaves used to hang from chains and ain't much changed, it's in the
game
Race is umm, race is umm, racism... we're being overrun
Guns in the hands of racist sons – drawn...
They sketch us even before the slave catchers can catch us
I may not fit the description of a serial killer but...
There's already a serial number waiting, a cellmate, a gravesite
They've got to keep my DNA stranded, keep their chains tight
They fear that one day we may get our aim right
Like If all our city gangs learned to hang right...
So, unlike the branches of our past and present gravesites
That fruit would be strange... right

No Laughing Matters

For the icebreaker... I'm going to tell a couple of jokes... ready??
Dylan Roof follows 9 Black People into a Church...
No, no it goes...
4 Klansmen, 4 little Black Girls and 19 sticks of dynamite enter a church in Birmingham
No, Damn.. I hate crime (a hate crime)
Ok, Ok
1 Black Wallstreet in Tulsa, runs into White Supremacy... Fuck!!
That one always burns me up...
Alright, Ok, K, K – I've got it
1 Black Civilian, 1 White Cop at the wrong apartment, No
4 Cops on the beat, meet... Rodney King, WAIT...
It's 4 Cops, 41 shots and 1 Amadou Diallo – case enters a courtroom, NOPE
Let's throw that out
Oh, Ohhhh 4 Cops, 1 Black Man stand outside a Liquor Store
No, no...
1 Black Teen, 1 Asshole and a bag of skittles all take a walk, ARRGH,
Forgot the tea, I always get that one twisted
Oh, here it is... Oscar Grant catches bullet train at Fruitville Station,
No..wait, lemme get it right
Ok, picture this... 1492, 3 ships, smallpox...
Nah, that's not how it goes
Yes, yes a Black Man and a White Man both lose their uniform for taking a knee, both wonder... "What's Next (necks)!
Uh huh, Uh huh, N.F.L, Not Fucking Lying
Alright, Alright – Handcuffed Black Man shoots himself in the head while in Police custody
Just Kidding, that's like... impossible, right
Ok, so 1 Wall, hundreds of fences and thousands of Immigrants, No???
Democracy!!! Lol
Naw, for real this time, here it goes...
"Whites Only Men and Boys" Club makes decision on "Women's bodies" now everybody bitchin
Ok, Ok, here's a real joke
111

Richard White

What do you call 535 stopped up toilets? – Congressional Seats! (Ha ha ha)

I'm just trying to shed some light at the end of the tunnel where the shit funnels...
I'm just trying to hold on to my dignity, knowing they ended slavery just to hang me from a bigger tree, Bigotry
Niggas snicker when they don't get the bigger picture
Ignorance is simpler, commune with the cripplers
Get hung like fixtures and ornaments, pine – boxes, tress, all the same
It's all a game
Walk in your shame trying to laugh away the pain, like it hasn't left a stain...
On white sheets, loose leaf...
Like Laws, dot, Amendments, dot Declaration of Independence, Stop
Doctrine doesn't demand these devils deal better hands to the Field Hands
They're mocking We, mockery, apostrophe, got mouths to feed and housing needs
So, I'm about my business – enemy of the BBB...
"Bad Boys in Blue" not the Better Business Bureau
Too often we get, read rights, blew away
Respect the Red, White and Blue you say, Do You Say
Compliance is defiance when not a part of the alliance
They're firing more than they're hiring, like us expiring is inspiring
Ain't no humor in being human if you're this hue... Man
Nothing changes, they claim us dangerous and in need to train us, chain us, or cage us
As if our Peaceful Protests would've become riots if not met by their violence
Or when our, "I can't Breathe" is taken as a joke
Every time another black Man is choked, hung by his throat, suffocated by hope... Nope
It's not amusing to the Republic
But I bet they're hilarious when in private...
Lemme stop with the jokes before they become offensive, and just take a moment... of silence

*Seriously...
    it's a joke,
        right?

113

Crown

I am the head, the Mane-land
Strands of stranded strangers came to tame man, they can't...
Take up aim and claimed lives, names, wives, slaves
Filled graves, ships
I think, I twist, coil, I kink
They press, attempt to straighten me out, cause breakage, lie
Trying not to die (dye) we bind, they split ends
Chopping heads, shed – blood, floods, runs
Parts seas (sees) dark skin
I am home
They search, comb, picks our young, kidnaps
Drags fro across waves, ceased, taken in
Bend over, bending backwards
Onto life, clenching, holding, braiding arms onto hope
Around necks, braided ropes, families torn
I am the form of babies being born, we must guard them
Roots, seeds, to be born, adorn, grow
Flowers, gardens, corn rows, plats
I am thorns wrapped across temples and brow, mounted
I am mountain, unscalable, un-scathed come unfavorable actions
I am blackness, galaxies, they only see my Suns (sons)...
As a resource, source of life, energy
Giver of life to an enemy
Our enemies hurt me, burn me, never deserve, or earn me
Stolen, shamed, claimed only to be renamed as their gain
I am pain pouring, I am both war and peace
I am as fast as sleep, elder than light or life
Powerful enough to conquer sight, and sound, absorb...
I am Mother of all shades and colors, they only exist in I
Father of pigment, the melanin inside, I am both humility and pride
They wish to divide, pry, rip into
I am that encaged rage that occupies the mind and rent is due
They pay – close attention, watch me
I am fuel and flame, ember, I remember
Every Knuckle, Knife and Knee
As they Knocked over Kingdoms Killing Kids belonging to me

115

Richard White

Every Kiss Kept Knotting Knots in nooses on necks, I Know
They wish to own me
I am Crown, regal
Never meant to sit upon or rest
I stand – on top the Messenger, the Prophets, the Rulers
I bang, front lines, I hunt, climb up, rise
Reach, come heat, I blow out
Every cut, I brush off, shadows may fade
I am always new growth, like Lambswool, deeply rooted
Arms stretched, held high, hung
Desired enough for worship by some
A blend of blushes, beiges, blondes, bronzes, blacks, and browns
I am the Crown

This Black

This black is more than colored flags and hand gestures
This black, this that black blood of our ancestors
Ancient civilizations forged into crippled nations of repainted
pictures, tainted pagan scriptures
Politics and parlor tricks performed perfectly by the Parliaments
Some of us swallowed it, followed it and became a part of it
But not this black, this black...
This that if mother, father, son ain't your trinity
You've been learning the meaning of "Family" whilst listening to your
enemy
Daughter, Sister, Queen Supreme, if you've forgotten that, stop that
This black, this that, "Hi, I'm different" Hieroglyphic, high uplifted
Knocked down by those I've uplifted
Some would rather enslavement over saving, so they kill their saviors,
their aim is different
This that black that those who lack it can't stand to sit with
This that black that can't forget shit
This that black they couldn't crack with crack though it brought a
cancer with it, an epidemic
This that black born of Mother Henrietta Lacks and a handsome nigga
That child prodigy, physics, and philosophy
That black they'd rather misinform and lie to me than to sharpen me
They'd rather harden me, an attempt to trap the god in me
This that melanin momma made music with
Muse to movements with, mixed moonlight with midnight and made
many
Mouths to feed, she fed plenty
This black, this that Spook before there was a door to sit by
This that black that'll do more than get by
That black that'd rather be real than to be rich
This that black that fought back when Willie lynched
This black, this that black that won't whistle for attention, another
lynching an open casket
My kin, overrun with bastards cause our skin has labeled our fathers
as hazards
I guess being a black parent is a job to die for
117

Richard White

This black, this that fuck what you've heard, I'm 5/3 (five thirds), superb
Superior, supreme, all-encompassing and in between, kings and queens
That Alpha and Omega, that apex, omnipotent, Son I shine
Like a million solar soldiers' souls
This black, this that somewhere between Algeria and Zimbabwe is my home
Abyssinian to Zulu in my bones, warrior people
For wherever I roam becomes my throne, architecture
This black, this that authority to author it
A prophet who knows his enemy profited when they stole his freedom and began to market it is often targeted for being talkative
So into the Hawk it is, sit high, wings rounded
Pure predator at heart, prey(pray), stay grounded
No matter how enticing and inviting their truth sounded
Its roots browning like the soil it's housed in
This that black founded on every "fuck you" given in return for our forgiving and forgetting
This that black that figured out your prisons and systems of oppression
And how you abuse your power as a weapon
This black is as deep as the hole you dug when our people pleaded for peace like we owed you blood
This that "live for, die for, kill for those I love"
This black, this that black that hits back like whiplash and whip lashings for your crookedness
Killings and kidnappings for control
You called it colonialism and Christianity
Quantities of color-coated white lies you've handed me
This that, this black, this that pitch black, African booty-scratching, porch-monkey about to go ape shit
This that retaliation for the rape and hate trapped aboard your slave ships
The treachery you got away with and the bullshit you claim to make America Great with
Every day the same shit
This black, this that black that's going to change it

119

Richard White

#MAKING POETS IMMORTAL

310 BROWN STREET ™

PUBLISHING

310brownstreet.com

Scan for more from Shake...

Richard White

www.ingramcontent.com/pod-product-compliance
Lightning Source LLC
Chambersburg PA
CBHW060543100426
42742CB00013B/2434